Original title:
Rising with Grace

Copyright © 2024 Swan Charm
All rights reserved.

Author: Liisi Lendorav
ISBN HARDBACK: 978-9916-89-706-5
ISBN PAPERBACK: 978-9916-89-707-2
ISBN EBOOK: 978-9916-89-708-9

The Lifting of the Soul's Veil

In the quiet whispers of the night,
Hearts awaken to the ethereal light.
Veils of sorrow gently unfurl,
As love aligns with the cosmic swirl.

In prayerful silence, spirits rise,
Reaching up towards the endless skies.
Veils lifted, revealing the divine,
Unity flows through space and time.

Eyes closed in trust, the journey starts,
Lifting burdens, with open hearts.
The veil dissolves, grace takes hold,
In sacred warmth, our stories unfold.

Every tear becomes a song,
A melody where we all belong.
In the sacred space, we ascend,
The soul's veil lifted, love's pure blend.

Climbing Towards Celestial Embrace

With every step upon the earth,
We seek the place of holy birth.
Climbing higher, hearts ablaze,
In the light, we lost the maze.

The mountain calls, our spirits soar,
Each breath whispers of ancient lore.
In struggle and joy, we ascend,
Towards the arms of love, our friend.

With faith as guide, we shall not fall,
Responding to that sacred call.
The weight of doubt, we cast aside,
In unity, we climb with pride.

Each summit reached, a blessing bright,
In the embrace of the holy light.
Through trials faced, our souls refine,
In celestial arms, we intertwine.

Illuminated by the Sacred Flame

In the stillness, the flame glows bright,
A beacon of hope in the darkest night.
Hearts aflame with divine grace,
Illuminated by love's embrace.

In the dance of shadows and light,
The sacred flame shines ever bright.
Casting warmth on the coldest fears,
It ignites faith as it reappears.

From ashes rise, the spirit's call,
The flame unites, embracing all.
In its glow, burdens fall away,
Guiding souls towards a brand new day.

Seek the flame within your heart,
Let it guide you, a holy art.
In every flicker, life's embrace,
Illuminated by the sacred grace.

The Dance of Hope Above

In the heavens, the stars align,
A cosmic dance, the truth divine.
Hope glimmers softly in the dark,
A celestial symphony, ignites the spark.

Angelic whispers fill the air,
As we partake in this grand affair.
In every heartbeat, joy resides,
In unity, our spirit glides.

With every twirl, the world shall sway,
To the rhythm of love, we find our way.
Beneath the heavens, forever free,
The dance of hope, in harmony.

Through trials faced, we rise anew,
In hope's embrace, we find what's true.
So let us dance beneath the sky,
With hope above, our spirits fly.

Where Hope Touches the Sky

In the dawn's gentle light, we rise,
Hearts aflame with desire to fly.
Faith like an anchor, firm and wise,
Whispers of promise in the sky.

Each step forward, a dance with grace,
Guided by love, with every trace.
In trials, find strength to embrace,
Hope blooms brightly in every place.

Through valleys deep and mountains tall,
The spirit soars, it will not fall.
With every heartbeat, heed the call,
Where hope touches life, we stand as all.

The Alchemy of Faith's Uplift

In shadows cast by doubt's cruel hand,
The gold of faith begins to glow.
Each sorrow molded, a sacred strand,
Transformed by love, in ebb and flow.

With quiet prayers and whispered dreams,
We weave a fabric of the Divine.
Every tear, a river of streams,
Turned to blessings, our spirits shine.

Let burdens lift as we believe,
And mountains crumble in the light.
In the heart's furnace, we perceive,
The alchemy of faith so bright.

Beneath the Infinite Canopy

Under the stars, we gather tight,
In wonder, we gaze at heaven's dome.
Each twinkling light a beacon bright,
Reminding us, we're never alone.

Beneath the canopy, we're one,
Bound by threads of love and grace.
In the quiet night, our hearts run,
Toward the promise of a warm embrace.

With every sigh, we lift our prayer,
Carried by winds of tender care.
In unity found, we freely share,
A tapestry woven, rich and rare.

To the Tapestry of Exaltation

Threads of joy in colors bright,
Woven tight in sacred dance.
Every joy, a fleeting light,
Every trial a chance to enhance.

In the loom of life, we find our song,
A melody where spirits connect.
Through every heart, we all belong,
In love's embrace, we stand, reflect.

To the rhythm of faith, our hands do play,
Creating beauty from whispers of trust.
In exaltation, we find our way,
Together lifted, our souls combust.

Voices of Renewal

In quiet whispers of the morn,
We seek the strength to be reborn.
Every prayer, a gentle sigh,
Life takes flight, our spirits high.

Among the trees, hope softly grows,
In sacred spaces, love bestows.
Each step forward, grace bestowed,
Together, we traverse this road.

With every heartbeat, wisdom rings,
The song of life, the joy it brings.
Through trials faced, we find our way,
Illuminated by the day.

The sun will rise on every face,
Uniting all in warm embrace.
In harmony, our hearts unite,
Voices rise to seek the light.

So let us sing in joyful praise,
For in this journey, love displays.
Hand in hand, we walk as one,
In the arms of the Holy Son.

Radiant Horizons

Beyond the hills where daylight gleams,
Lie dreams of faith and tender themes.
With open hearts, we boldly stand,
To seek the touch of God's own hand.

In azure skies, the angels glide,
Guiding souls on this great ride.
With every dawn, a chance to see,
The radiant light of harmony.

Through valleys low and mountains high,
We lift our eyes, prepared to fly.
In every breath, the promise clear,
With faith, we cast aside our fear.

The world awakens, bright and new,
Each heart ignites, a vibrant hue.
Together, we shall walk this path,
Embracing love that ever lasts.

As shadows fade and hope appears,
Our hearts will dance, erase the fears.
With every step, a joyful song,
To radiant horizons, we belong.

A Journey Towards the Light

Upon the road where shadows fade,
We carry hope, not dismayed.
Each moment spent, a lesson learned,
In every heart, a fire burned.

We walk on trails both wide and narrow,
With faith that fuels our daily sparrow.
In fellowship, we find our way,
A journey blessed with light of day.

Through storms that test our weary souls,
We cling to visions, our sacred goals.
With courage strong and spirits bright,
We travel forth towards the light.

The stars above, a guide so true,
Illuminating paths anew.
In every step, we hear the call,
Together, we will never fall.

A promise held in every heart,
In unity, we never part.
For on this journey, hand in hand,
We find our purpose, hearts will stand.

Hearts in the Hands of the Divine

With every prayer, our spirits lift,
In sacred moments, we receive a gift.
Hearts entwined in love's embrace,
In the arms of grace, we find our space.

The river flows, a gentle guide,
Through every trial, we abide.
In storms we face, we hear the rhyme,
A whisper soft, transcending time.

As seasons change, our souls ignite,
In every shadow, seek the light.
Together bound, a tapestry,
Hearts in the hands of the Divine, we'll be.

With open hearts, we break the chain,
Finding beauty in each pain.
In every lesson, wisdom grows,
In faith, the seeds of love we sow.

Let joy abound, let sorrows cease,
Together we shall find our peace.
In every moment, love's design,
We are the hearts in hands divine.

Wings of Devotion

In the silence, hearts ignite,
Faith like flames, burning bright.
With every prayer, a whispered sigh,
We reach for heaven, ever nigh.

In the stillness, spirits soar,
Guided by love, we seek the more.
In sacred bonds, our souls entwine,
In every tear, a spark divine.

Through trials faced, we learn to trust,
In grace bestowed, we rise from dust.
With wings of hope, our burdens lifted,
In every prayer, a life gifted.

Together we walk, hand in hand,
In unity, we make our stand.
With hearts ablaze, our voices sing,
To the heavens, our praises ring.

In the morning light, we seek the way,
With kindness sown, we greet the day.
In the depths of night, we find our peace,
In wings of devotion, our love won't cease.

From Shadows to Blessed Heights

From the shadows, the soul takes flight,
Yearning for wisdom, seeking light.
In the valleys, we learn to rise,
With faith as our guide, we touch the skies.

Through whispered doubts, we find our song,
In every heartache, we grow strong.
From ashes born, our spirits gleam,
In the fabric of life, we weave our dream.

Upward we climb, with eyes aglow,
Casting aside all fear and woe.
In moments bleak, our faith ignites,
We journey forth to blessed heights.

With every step, love leads the way,
In gratitude's arms, we love and pray.
From the darkness, we emerge anew,
Bathed in blessings, our spirits true.

In unity bound, we face the dawn,
From shadows past, our fears are gone.
With open hearts, we share our flight,
In the embrace of divine delight.

Sacred Ascent of the Heart

In the stillness, echoes resound,
The sacred ascent is where love is found.
With each heartbeat, a message flows,
In the depths of silence, the spirit grows.

Through trials faced, our faith we crave,
In the waves of grace, we learn to save.
With each gesture, kindness is sown,
In the garden of hope, love is grown.

On the mountain high, souls intertwine,
In the sacred dance, our paths align.
The ascent is steep, the journey long,
But united in love, we have grown strong.

In whispers soft, the truth revealed,
In the warmth of faith, our wounds are healed.
Step by step, we rise from the night,
In the sacred ascent, we find our light.

With eyes uplifted, we seek the divine,
In the embrace of love, our hearts combine.
The journey unfolds, our spirits take part,
In the sacred ascent of the heart.

Clarity in the Clouds of Spirit

In the clouds of spirit, we soar high,
To realms unseen, on wings we fly.
Amidst the shadows, clarity reigns,
In the whispers of heaven, joy sustains.

Through storms that thunder, we find our peace,
In silent moments, worries cease.
With faith as our anchor, we stand tall,
In the light of love, we find our call.

With each new dawn, the world ignites,
In every heart, the divine invites.
With clarity gained, we seek to know,
The paths of light where blessings flow.

In every journey, we learn and grow,
In the clouds of spirit, love we sow.
Together we rise, hand in hand,
In the embrace of grace, we make our stand.

With eyes wide open, we chase the sun,
In the clouds of spirit, our hearts are one.
Together we dance, in joy we share,
In clarity found, we're lost in prayer.

Ascend with Light

In the dawn's embrace, we rise,
Casting shadows to the skies.
With each step, our spirits soar,
Guided by the love we pour.

Beneath the stars, our hearts unite,
In the presence of holy light.
The path is steep, but grace ensures,
In faith we walk, our souls secure.

With every breath, the sacred call,
Echoes softly, never small.
Through trials faced, we gain our sight,
Aligning hearts to purest light.

As mountains shift and rivers bend,
We find our way, the weary mend.
Together bound, we gain our breath,
In life, in death, we are the faith.

So lift your eyes to heaven's glow,
Let spirit's flame within you flow.
In unity, we raise our might,
To ascend with love, to rise in light.

Echoes of the Divine Path

Upon the road, His footsteps tread,
Whispers of truth along we spread.
Through valleys low, and peaks so high,
His voice, a guide that will not die.

In quiet moments, hearts will see,
The love that flows, undeniably.
Each echo leads, a gentle sign,
Reminding us of the divine.

Through trials fierce, through doubt and pain,
We find our strength, our hope again.
For every step in shadows cast,
The light will shine, the die is cast.

With every sunset, every dawn,
The journey brings us ever on.
A sacred path, though worn and long,
In faith, together we belong.

So walk with love, let kindness reign,
For in this grace, we'll break the chain.
With open hearts, we will embrace,
The echoes of His boundless grace.

Ascension's Gentle Whisper

In stillness found, the spirit sings,
Of love and grace in all good things.
A gentle whisper in the night,
Guides weary souls toward the light.

With open hearts, we seek the dawn,
From shadows deep, we are reborn.
The path to joy, though sometimes steep,
Calls us to rise, to boldly leap.

In every trial, there's a chance,
To find the spark, to join the dance.
With every tear, a lesson learned,
In every flame, our hearts are burned.

So listen close to heaven's call,
Let not the weight of doubt enthrall.
For in the quiet, hope will rise,
And in our faith, we touch the skies.

Each step a prayer, each breath a song,
Together we'll find where we belong.
In ascension's gentle, loving grace,
We'll find our strength to embrace our place.

Wings of Faith Unfurled

Like eagles soaring, bold and free,
Our spirits lift in unity.
With wings of faith, we rise above,
Embracing all, with endless love.

Through storms and trials, we must endure,
For every heart, the light is sure.
In whispered prayers, we find our way,
And trust the dawn will greet the day.

In sacred stillness, truth unfolds,
As ancient stories, new ones told.
Together bound, we chase the light,
Transforming shadows into bright.

So let each soul unfurl its wing,
And in our hearts, let joy take wing.
With every step, we touch the sky,
In faith, in love, we soar on high.

Together on this journey grand,
We rise above, we take a stand.
With wings of faith forever twirled,\nWe find our place within the world.

Celestial Vine

In the garden where the light shines,
The celestial vine entwines with grace.
Each leaf a whisper of divine signs,
Our spirits rise in this sacred space.

Hidden fruits that bear sweet promise,
Nourish the soul with love's embrace.
In shadows deep, they find solace,
In every heart, God's warm trace.

Sing praises to the Holy Light,
Each dawn brings blessings from above.
With every prayer, we take flight,
United in faith, we share His love.

Through trials faced, our spirits bloom,
As branches stretch towards the skies.
In His warmth, we will not gloom,
For in our hearts, true hope lies.

Bound by roots, we grow as one,
In the presence of the heavenly dew.
We walk in faith towards the sun,
With love and light, our burdens slew.

Elysium Awaits

In the sigh of winds, a promise flows,
Elysium awaits in the quiet night.
With every star, a glimpse that shows,
The path to peace, the way to light.

In fields of gold, the angels tread,
Where dreams intertwine with joy and grace.
With each step forward, fears shed,
We seek the dawn; we find our place.

Heavenly choruses sing our song,
In unity, our spirits soar.
With faith as wings, we grow strong,
Elysium awaits at heaven's door.

In gentle whispers, truth unfolds,
Every heart a lantern bright.
Together, we embrace the bold,
And journey forth into the light.

As prisms cast their vibrant hue,
Each moment blessed in divine share.
Elysium awaits for me and you,
With love and faith beyond compare.

The Veil of Triumph

In shadows cast by doubt and fear,
The veil of triumph softly glows.
With strength that rises, crystal clear,
Our spirits bend, but never close.

Through trials faced and burdens borne,
We learn to dance amidst the strife.
In every heart, a crown is worn,
Our faith, a light, gives strength to life.

Each challenge met with steadfast grace,
A tapestry of courage spun.
In prayer, we find our sacred space,
The battles fought, the races run.

The veil lifts high, the dawn breaks free,
Our eyes behold the radiant sky.
In unity, we find our key,
With lifted hearts, we learn to fly.

Let joy be known in every cheer,
Together rising, hand in hand.
Through love and hope, we hold so dear,
The veil of triumph across the land.

In the Shelter of Grace

In the shelter of grace, we find our peace,
Where love envelops like a tender breeze.
With every sigh, our worries cease,
In sacred embrace, our spirits please.

Under Heaven's watchful gaze,
We gather strength from bonds unbroken.
Through every storm and darkened phase,
In whispered prayers, our hearts have spoken.

In quiet moments, faith ignites,
As blessings flow from every tear.
In the stillness of starry nights,
We feel the presence always near.

With every trial, we rise anew,
In the arms of mercy, we stand strong.
Together, every path we'll pursue,
In the shelter of grace, we belong.

In love's soft light, we cast our fears,
Hand in hand, we journey far.
With hopeful hearts, we'll dry our tears,
In the shelter of grace, we are.

The Serene Climb

In quietude, I tread the way,
Each step a prayer, in light of day.
The path ascends, so steep and high,
With faith as wings, I learn to fly.

Above the clouds, my spirit soars,
Through whispered truths, eternity roars.
In every breath, the sacred grace,
I find within this holy place.

The mountain's call, my heart obeys,
In nature's arms, my soul it stays.
With love that binds, the journey's peace,
In stillness where all struggles cease.

Each rock and stone, a tale to tell,
Of seekers past, who knew Him well.
With grace they climbed, their burdens shed,
In harmony, where angels tread.

And when I reach that summit high,
I lift my gaze to endless sky.
With every heartbeat, I shall sing,
In union with the Lord, our King.

Embracing the Celestial Dawn

With every dawn, the light breaks free,
A chorus sung, in harmony.
In morning's grace, I feel the rise,
Awake my soul, to search the skies.

The sun's embrace, a warm caress,
In golden rays, I find my rest.
Each moment pure, a sacred gift,
In silence deep, my spirit lifts.

Through fields of light, I wander forth,
The whispers call from heaven's north.
In gentle breezes, wisdom flows,
Where peace abounds and love bestows.

A canvas vast, the heavens glow,
With colors bright, a holy show.
I raise my hands in gratitude,
For every grace and solitude.

To walk in faith, with heart aligned,
In every moment, love defined.
The dawn shall come, a promise true,
Embrace the light, begin anew.

Heart's Elevation in Sacred Silence

In stillness deep, my heart shall rise,
To realms unseen, beyond the skies.
In whispered prayers, I find the way,
Where sacred silence holds the sway.

A hush profound, the world fades fast,
Each breath, a bond with love that lasts.
In quiet grace, my spirit learns,
To seek the truth, the fire burns.

In solitude, the soul takes flight,
In holy shadows, I find light.
A gentle nudge, the heart's own song,
In purest thought, where I belong.

The universe, a sacred space,
Where every heartbeat shows His grace.
In every moment, wisdom streams,
In silent whispers, life redeems.

The elevation of the heart,
A journey shared, we are the part.
With every sigh, a step toward peace,
In sacred silence, love's release.

Journey to the Sacred Summit

The path unwinds, a sacred quest,
To climb the heights where spirits rest.
With every step, my heartbeats soar,
In faith, I seek forevermore.

The mountains rise, like pillars proud,
Inviting me beneath their shroud.
In nature's arms, I find my guide,
Through trials faced, with God beside.

Amid the rocks, the echoes dwell,
Of love and truths, a timeless spell.
With every view, a glimpse of grace,
The heavens call, my soul's embrace.

With open heart, I tread the ground,
In sacred steps, the lost are found.
The summit calls, a mystic dance,
In every heartbeat lies the chance.

To reach the heights, where blessings flow,
In unity, our spirits grow.
The journey ends, yet starts anew,
In love divine, our hearts be true.

Ascendant Spirit

In silent prayer we rise,
With hearts that seek the light,
Guided by His grace,
Our spirits take to flight.

The heavens open wide,
Embracing souls anew,
In unity we stand,
Our faith to see us through.

Through trials we will soar,
Our burdens laid aside,
With hope that lights the dark,
In Him we shall abide.

The path is ever bright,
With love that knows no end,
In every whispered prayer,
Our spirits shall ascend.

From earthly ties we rise,
To realms beyond the veil,
With every breath we take,
His promise shall not fail.

Blossoms of the Beloved

In gardens of the heart,
The petals softly sway,
Each blossom tells a tale,
Of love that won't decay.

With each dawn that breaks,
The colors find their hue,
In every fragrant sigh,
The love reveals what's true.

Through trials like the storms,
Our roots grow deep and strong,
In faith we find the strength,
To rise where we belong.

The sweetest songs arise,
From every whispered prayer,
In unity we bloom,
With love beyond compare.

So let the blossoms speak,
Of grace in every tear,
In the garden of His heart,
Our souls forever near.

In the Shelter of the Almighty

In shadows we find peace,
A refuge from the storm,
With faith like gentle wings,
Our hearts begin to warm.

The shelter of His arms,
A fortress for our soul,
In trials and in fears,
He makes our spirits whole.

Through waters deep and wide,
He walks beside us still,
In every whispered prayer,
Our hearts are freed from will.

In quietude we rest,
A balm for every pain,
In the shelter of His love,
We rise to shine again.

With every step we take,
We find our path made clear,
In the shelter of the Almighty,
Our peace is ever near.

Echoes of Divine Love

In the stillness of the night,
His love begins to sing,
An echo through the dark,
Of hope that He will bring.

With every gentle breeze,
His whispers fill the air,
A melody of grace,
Reminding us He's there.

The stars reflect His light,
As guides upon our way,
In every shining glance,
His love will never stray.

In valleys low and wide,
His voice will lead us on,
With echoes of His truth,
Our journey has begun.

In every heart's refrain,
His love will not depart,
An echo of the divine,
Resounding in each heart.

The Promise of Tomorrow

In the dawn's embrace we rise,
Hope ignites with every sigh.
Faith, a lantern in the dark,
Guides our hearts to the sky.

Each moment teems with grace,
Whispers of a love so true.
With every step, we find our way,
A path illuminated anew.

Storms may gather up ahead,
Yet we stand firm, hand in hand.
For in unity, we are strong,
Together, we shall stand.

Beneath the heavens wide and vast,
Promises like stars do shine.
In each trial, we learn and grow,
The future yours and mine.

So trust in what is yet to come,
For tomorrow holds great light.
With faith as our steadfast shield,
We walk toward the bright.

Reflections of the Creator

In quiet woods, the beauty speaks,
Whispers of the Maker's will.
Every leaf and gentle stream,
A canvas of love, calm and still.

Mountains rise with majesty,
Skyward, touching heaven's gate.
In their shadows, we seek truth,
Embers of a divine fate.

Stars twinkle in the night,
Messages from far away.
In their glow, we find our worth,
Guidance through the darkened fray.

The ocean's song, a sacred hymn,
Rolling waves in timeless dance.
Echoes of the heart's desire,
Inviting every soul to glance.

So pause and look around with awe,
Feel the pulse of creation's heart.
In every breath, a gift unfolds,
From the One who gave us art.

Stepping Stones of Faith

Life's journey requires a map,
Each step a potent prayer.
On stones of faith, we gently tread,
Trusting in the Lord's care.

Hand in hand, we forge our way,
Through valleys deep and wide.
With each challenge, we learn strength,
In Him, we do abide.

Moments shared on winding paths,
A tapestry of grace.
In the love and laughter shared,
We find our sacred space.

Though shadows may loom large and near,
The light shall break the dawn.
With every trial, we rise with hope,
From night, we are reborn.

So let us walk with open hearts,
With faith as our embrace.
Each stone a testament of trust,
In His eternal grace.

Echoes in the Stillness

In the silence, whispers grow,
Messages from the divine.
Gentle echoes calling forth,
Hearts entwined in sacred rhyme.

Through the stillness, love and peace,
Wrap around us like a cloak.
Every breath a prayer of hope,
In the quiet, hearts awake.

In the pause, we hear the call,
A soft echo of pure light.
Guiding souls through darkest nights,
To new beginnings, pure and bright.

In reflection, we seek the truth,
In silence, answers start to flow.
For in the calm, we feel His grace,
In every heartbeat, love we know.

So let the stillness guide our way,
In faith, we find our rest.
For in the echoes of the night,
We dwell in blessings, truly blessed.

The Dawn of New Beginnings

In the hush of morn's first light,
Hope awakens, shining bright.
The shadows fade, the sun appears,
Washing away our doubts and fears.

With each breath, we find relief,
A promise held, a seed of belief.
Faith ignites, guiding our way,
Through fields of grace, come what may.

Each step unfolds a sacred path,
Where love abounds and trials pass.
In unity, our spirits rise,
Under the vast and open skies.

Embrace the journey, feel the call,
For in His light, we'll never fall.
Through valleys deep and mountains high,
We walk with purpose, ever nigh.

At dawn's embrace, our hearts will sing,
For every ending, new beginnings bring.
In faith we trust, in love we stand,
Guided by His gentle hand.

Embracing Divine Whispers

In silence deep, the heart will hear,
The gentle voice that calms our fear.
Through trials faced and storms that rage,
God's whispers guide from age to age.

Each moment spent in quiet prayer,
Lifts burdens high, our souls laid bare.
His wisdom flows like morning dew,
Refreshing hearts with love so true.

As branches stretch toward skies above,
We seek the source of endless love.
Through every breath, we feel the grace,
Of sacred light, a warm embrace.

With open hearts, we shall receive,
The gifts of peace that God conceived.
In unity, our spirits soar,
Forever anchored on His shore.

In divine whispers, truth revealed,
In lives transformed, His love is sealed.
With faith in hand, we traverse the night,
Towards the dawn, a guiding light.

Ascent of the Soul

From depths of earth to heights unknown,
The spirit rises, freely flown.
With every step, the heart ignites,
In search of truth, amidst the lights.

Each trial faced, a stone turned gold,
In love's embrace, the brave and bold.
With strength bestowed from grace above,
We journey forth, sustained by love.

In mountain's shadow, wisdom calls,
Amidst the echoes, our spirit thralls.
Through storms and sun, in faith we'll stand,
Holding tight to His guiding hand.

With eyes alight and hearts ablaze,
We rise to sing of endless praise.
Each dawn unfolds a brighter view,
The soul ascends, forever true.

The climb is steep, the path is wide,
But in His arms, we shall abide.
Towards the skies, our voices blend,
In love's embrace, we transcend.

A Pilgrim's Journey

With humble heart, the pilgrim sets,
Upon a road where love begets.
A path of faith, through joys and strife,
Finding solace in the dance of life.

With every step, the spirit yearns,
For wisdom gained, each lesson learned.
In unity, we walk along,
Together lifted, ever strong.

The winding trails, both rough and smooth,
Mirror the story that we prove.
Through valleys low and mountains grand,
We hold the light, a guiding hand.

In every face, a glimpse of grace,
The sacred presence we embrace.
For in this journey, hearts will mend,
And every stranger be a friend.

So onward, pilgrim, never cease,
Embrace the trials; find your peace.
For in each moment, love's refrain,
From start to end, we rise again.

Heavenly Bloom

In gardens where angels tread with grace,
Petals unfold in soft embrace.
Colors dance beneath the sun,
Whispering songs of everyone.

With every bud, a promise made,
In sacred joy, our fears will fade.
The fragrance lifts to skies above,
A sacred hymn of hope and love.

Each morning brings a fresh bouquet,
Nature's art in bright array.
As petals share their sweet perfume,
We find our hearts in heaven's bloom.

The gentle rain, a blessing true,
Nourishing soil, life starts anew.
In eternal cycles, we believe,
In the garden, we shall weave.

So let us wander hand in hand,
Through this divine, enchanted land.
With every step, a prayer we claim,
In heavenly bloom, we love his name.

Steps into Eternity

With each small step, the path unfolds,
A journey whispered through the folds.
Footprints left in sacred ground,
In faith, we walk, love all around.

A light ahead, so warm and bright,
It guides us through the dark of night.
In every heartbeat, grace is found,
As heaven's melodies resound.

Time drifts softly like a prayer,
With every breath, we know he's there.
As moments fade, the spirit soars,
Into forever, love restores.

With angels' wings, we'll rise above,
In unity, we find our love.
Each step we take, a promise true,
In eternity, we're born anew.

So let us walk this blessed road,
In every heart, a sacred code.
Together bound, with souls aligned,
Steps into eternity, intertwined.

The Blessing of Each Sunrise

Awake, arise, the dawn appears,
A blessing wrapped in golden layers.
The sun ascends to kiss the earth,
Celebrating life, our daily birth.

Soft whispers dance on morning breeze,
Each new day brings us to our knees.
In gratitude, we lift our voice,
In light, we bloom, we rejoice.

The sky a canvas, painted bright,
A masterpiece of love and light.
With every ray, a gentle start,
The sun reflects our longing heart.

As shadows flee and hope takes flight,
We walk in faith, guided by light.
With open arms, we greet the day,
In every moment, prayer will stay.

So let us cherish this divine sign,
The blessing of each sunrise, so fine.
With hearts united, we will share,
In every dawn, we find our prayer.

A Choir of Stars

In the night sky, so vast and deep,
A choir of stars begins to weep.
Each twinkle sings a song so bright,
Guiding lost souls through the night.

Heavenly voices from afar,
They lift our spirits, each shining star.
In their glow, we find our peace,
A promise that our doubts will cease.

When shadows fall and dreams take flight,
The stars compose, their chords unite.
With harmony, they weave the air,
In celestial love, we lay our care.

So gaze above with hearts aglow,
Find comfort there, let worries go.
In the night's embrace, a sacred chance,
To join the stars in a cosmic dance.

With every wish upon the light,
We sing with stars, in pure delight.
Together bound, through space and time,
A choir of stars, in endless rhyme.

The Light Beyond Shadows

In the still of night, hope glows bright,
Casting away fears, a guiding light.
From the depths of sorrow, we rise anew,
Touched by the light that forever shines through.

Through valleys of darkness, our spirits soar,
Embracing the love that opens the door.
Each step we take, a journey of grace,
Found in the solace of His warm embrace.

When doubts cloud our hearts, we seek the flame,
Whispers of comfort, calling His name.
With faith as our anchor, we stand tall,
For in the light, we are never too small.

Shadows may linger, but they cannot stay,
For the radiance of truth leads the way.
In each golden beam, our souls find rest,
In the arms of love, we are truly blessed.

Beyond every trial, a promise so clear,
The light of His presence casts out all fear.
Forever we journey, hand in hand, we find,
The light beyond shadows, forever entwined.

Transformation in the Quiet

In whispers of stillness, the heart learns to bend,
To change and to grow, like a lover's friend.
With patience we listen, to lessons so wise,
In the quiet of moments, our spirit will rise.

As dawn breaks the silence, new colors unfold,
Transforming our trials to treasures of gold.
Through the lens of His grace, we feel the divine,
A metamorphosis rare, like the finest of wine.

In the spaces of calm, we reclaim our sight,
Finding beauty in shadows, embracing the light.
Sudden revelations, like blossoms will bloom,
In the garden of peace, dispelling all gloom.

With each step of faith, we unravel the weave,
The tapestry woven with love to believe.
In transformation's embrace, we find who we are,
A journey of purpose, like a wish on a star.

Now, in the quiet, our souls take their flight,
Transformed by His love, we soar into the night.
Beneath starlit skies, our spirits rejoice,
In the silence of growth, we find our true voice.

Guided by Faith's Lantern

In the night of uncertainty, a light will appear,
Faith's lantern ignites, chasing away fear.
With every step taken, the path becomes clear,
Guided by love, we embrace what is near.

Through storms of confusion, we hold steady fast,
Knowing each challenge shall one day be passed.
With faith as our compass, we wander the way,
Finding strength in each moment, come what may.

In shadows that linger, the lantern shines bright,
Illuminating paths hidden from our sight.
With hearts intertwined, we venture as one,
Embracing the journey, till the race is won.

Every flicker of hope, a call to our souls,
Drawing us closer to love that consoles.
Together we march on, side by side we stand,
With faith's gentle whisper, we're led by His hand.

As dawn breaks the silence, our hearts sing anew,
For guided by faith, we know what is true.
With each passing moment, we find our way home,
Forever united, in love we will roam.

A Pathway of Serenity

In the garden of grace, we stroll hand in hand,
Finding peace in the whispers, where blessings expand.
Each step on this pathway, a melody sweet,
Leading us gently, with love at our feet.

Through valleys of trials, we learn to be still,
In moments of silence, we nurture the will.
With hearts open wide, and spirits set free,
We walk on this pathway, in love's unity.

As flowers unfold, in the warmth of the day,
Our souls connect deeply, in a vibrant array.
The fragrance of kindness where sorrows depart,
Each breath of serenity sings to the heart.

In twilight's embrace, we gather our dreams,
In the quiet of night, our spirit redeems.
With every soft whisper, and each gentle sigh,
We find our reflections, as stars fill the sky.

So let us walk onward, with faith as our guide,
In the pathway of serenity, forever abide.
For in each sacred moment, we find our true place,
Wrapped in the stillness, we're covered in grace.

Breathing in the Divine

In the silence, whispers call,
The sacred air, a gentle thrall.
Each breath a prayer, a sacred sign,
Awakening my soul, divine.

In morning light, the spirit wakes,
With every heartbeat, our love makes.
The world anew, in colors bright,
We find our way, with faith's pure light.

As evening falls, the shadows play,
Yet in our hearts, the light will stay.
With gratitude, our voices rise,
We sing our truth beneath the skies.

In every trial, a lesson learned,
Through darkest nights, our passion burned.
We share the light, we share the grace,
Finding unity in each embrace.

Breathing in the Divine, we see,
The beauty in our unity.
Together we stand, hand in hand,
In every heartbeat, we understand.

Lanterns on the Path

In the stillness of the night,
Lanterns glow with a gentle light.
Each flicker whispers tales of old,
Of faith and love, of hearts so bold.

Guiding souls through shadowed ways,
With every step, our spirits blaze.
Together woven, we journey on,
Embracing dawn, the dark is gone.

Each lantern shines with hope anew,
Illuminating paths we pursue.
In unity, we seek the grace,
Reflecting love in every place.

As we wander, hand in hand,
We weave a tapestry so grand.
In love's embrace, we find our start,
Guided by the light in our heart.

May our lanterns never fade,
In every moment, love displayed.
For on this path, together we'll roam,
Creating light, we find our home.

The Gift of Ascendancy

With every challenge, rises grace,
In trials faced, we find our place.
For every fall, there's strength found,
In whispered prayers, our souls unbound.

Ascendancy is not of pride,
But lifting others by our side.
In love's embrace, we rise and soar,
Together hearts forevermore.

With faith as wings, we will not tire,
Our spirits bold, our hearts on fire.
Through valleys deep and mountains high,
We reach for dreams that touch the sky.

As we rise, we share the light,
Each step we take, we banish night.
With open hearts, we journey on,
In the gift of love, we are reborn.

The gift of ascendancy we claim,
In truth, in love, we stake our name.
In unity, we find our song,
Together we belong, forever strong.

The Mosaic of Grace

In every shard, a story told,
A mosaic made from hearts of gold.
Each piece reflects a different hue,
Together forming something true.

With kindness stitched through trials faced,
We find the beauty in our haste.
In every crack, a light will shine,
Making all broken things divine.

From darkness blooms the fairest light,
Uniting souls, igniting sight.
In every heart, a sacred place,
We find our purpose in the grace.

Woven together, we stand tall,
In unity, we shall not fall.
In every moment, joy and pain,
We celebrate what love can gain.

The mosaic of grace, our shared delight,
Reflects the love in our steadfast flight.
In each connection, we embrace the space,
Creating beauty, we find our grace.

Glimpses of the Divine Cliff

In the whisper of dusk, grace unfurls,
Mirroring stars, the universe swirls.
Each shadow cast holds a sacred trace,
Divine light reveals in this tranquil space.

Mountains rise high, reaching for the dawn,
Each heartbeat echoes, a celestial song.
In silence, we witness, the truth so near,
Glimpses of glory, in faith, we steer.

With footsteps gentle upon hallowed ground,
Echos of love in creation abound.
Nature sings softly, a hymn to the heart,
In every creation, God's work of art.

As streams of light dance in the golden day,
Connecting our souls in a holy ballet.
We lift our eyes, seeking the sublime,
In moments of stillness, transcending time.

In the quiet embrace of night's tender glow,
Understanding deepens, as wonders show.
The Divine Cliff beckons, inviting our sight,
To gaze at the heavens, embracing the light.

Finding the Breath of Heaven

In the stillness of dawn, whispers arise,
Gentle breezes carry our heartfelt sighs.
With open souls, we yearn and we seek,
Finding the breath that makes our hearts speak.

Through valleys of doubt, where shadows conceal,
We wander in search of the truth we can feel.
The spirit awakens, igniting the flame,
In every moment, we honor His name.

With hands lifted high, we raise our praise,
Breath of heaven fills our soul's eager maze.
Each prayer ascends, a fragrant delight,
Finding connection in the sacred night.

In the chorus of life, where love intertwines,
Each heartbeat echoes the softest of signs.
With every step taken on this holy ground,
Finding the breath of heaven, we are bound.

Beneath the vast sky, our spirits take flight,
Embracing the wonders, basking in light.
In the dance of creation, we find our way,
Finding the breath of heaven, come what may.

Ascension of the Heart

In silence we gather, hearts open wide,
As echoes of truth in our spirits reside.
Through trials and joys, the journey unfolds,
Ascension of love, in the stories retold.

With each step we take, a promise is made,
In the strength of the spirit, fears start to fade.
In valleys so deep, hope rises like dawn,
Ascension of the heart, we rise and move on.

With wings made of dreams, and faith as our guide,
We traverse the mountains, with love at our side.
In unity's embrace, our destinies spark,
Lighting the shadows, igniting the dark.

Each heartbeat a prayer, a rhythm divine,
In the dance of the cosmos, our souls intertwine.
In sacred stillness, we cherish the art,
Ascension of the heart, where love plays its part.

Eternal connections, as layers unfold,
In all that we seek, the truth will be told.
With courage and grace, we tear the apart,
Embracing our journey, ascension of heart.

Wings of Celestial Light

In the dawn of our trust, we spread our wings,
Soaring on breezes that the spirit sings.
With every heartbeat, we claim our flight,
Wings of celestial light, a wondrous sight.

As clouds unfurl, revealing the blue,
We dance in the sun, with grace that's anew.
In the arms of the wind, we are set free,
Wings of celestial light, guiding our plea.

Through valleys of shadow, we journey with night,
Finding the path with our hearts burning bright.
In moments of silence, we hear the call,
Wings of celestial light, embracing us all.

With every ascent, fears start to dissolve,
In unity's chorus, we learn to evolve.
Each spirit ignites, love's luminous art,
Wings of celestial light, igniting the heart.

As stars wink above, we gather in cheer,
Holding each other, we conquer our fear.
With faith like the mountains, bold and upright,
Wings of celestial light, lifting us higher.

The Journey to Radiance

In valleys deep where shadows lie,
The heart seeks light, a flame on high.
With faith as compass, we shall roam,
In every step, we find our home.

Through deserts bare, our spirits soar,
With every challenge, we implore.
The dawn breaks clear, a guiding sign,
Towards love and grace, our souls align.

In waters pure, we wash away,
The burdens of the night and fray.
Beneath the stars, our hopes ignite,
Together we journey toward the light.

With open hearts and voices raised,
In unity, our lives are praised.
For in the struggle, bonds are formed,
In faith's embrace, our spirits warmed.

The journey holds both peace and strife,
Each trial brings a closer life.
With every step, we truly see,
The radiance of the One in me.

Celestial Transformations

From dust we rise, to stars we turn,
Through life's great dance, our souls will learn.
In each quiet breath, divinity,
Transforming us to what we're meant to be.

The night reveals a sky of grace,
Each constellation, a sacred space.
In cosmic echoes, we hear the call,
To rise above, to seek and know it all.

Wings unfurl, as spirits take flight,
In the stillness of the deepest night.
With radiant visions bright and true,
We awaken to a world anew.

In every prayer, a ripple spreads,
Uniting hearts, where love embeds.
Celestial whispers guide our way,
Towards the dawn of a brand new day.

As seasons shift and time unfolds,
The mystery of life gently holds.
In transformation, we find our place,
In cosmic embrace, we feel His grace.

Wings of the Spirit

On wings of peace, our spirits rise,
To touch the heavens, to claim the skies.
In whispers soft, the truth we hear,
A melody that calms our fear.

From mountains high to rivers wide,
We find His love, our faithful guide.
In every tear, a lesson learned,
In every joy, the heart discerned.

Through storms of doubt, we find our way,
With wings of faith, we learn to sway.
In unity, our voices blend,
On wings of hope, we shall ascend.

The light of dawn is drawing near,
As shadows fade, our path is clear.
Together, hand in hand we soar,
With wings of trust, forevermore.

In every heartbeat, grace abounds,
A sacred hymn in love resounds.
With wings of the spirit, we take flight,
Embracing the beauty of purest light.

Awakening to Providence

In quiet moments, hearts align,
With whispers soft, the truth shall shine.
As morning breaks and shadows flee,
Awakening to the grace we see.

With open eyes, we start to feel,
The sacred dance of the divine wheel.
In every breath, a sacred line,
Binding our souls to the grand design.

Through trials faced and paths not known,
We find in loss, the seeds are sown.
In being still, we learn to trust,
For providence, in Him, we must.

In every smile, in every tear,
We sense His presence drawing near.
In unity, together stand,
Awakening, guided by His hand.

The journey unfolds, a tapestry bright,
In every shadow, there glimmers light.
With hearts on fire and spirits free,
We awaken to our destiny.

Celestial Embrace

In skies adorned with heavenly light,
Angels gather, chorus bright.
Each whisper floats on sacred air,
Love unites us, pure and fair.

The stars align, a cosmic dance,
In every heart, a second chance.
Divine hands stretch from above,
Embracing all, a tapestry of love.

With every breath, the spirit sings,
In harmony with all living things.
The universe, a radiant embrace,
In this sacred, boundless space.

Trust the path that fate bestows,
In trials, grace forever flows.
Through hardship, joy shall rise,
To touch the heart and soul's skies.

Forever held in His embrace,
In gratitude, we seek His grace.
With open arms, we journey far,
Guided softly by a loving star.

The Heart's Horizon

Beneath the dawn, a whisper calls,
Hope awakens, rises over walls.
With every beat, a promise near,
Guiding souls from doubt and fear.

The sun ascends, a golden hue,
Painting skies with colors new.
In love and faith, we find our way,
To greet the light of another day.

The horizon speaks, a sacred truth,
In the eyes of the innocent youth.
Every glance, a glimpse divine,
Unfolding purpose, love's design.

Through valleys low and mountains high,
Our spirits soar, unyielded by.
In unity, we rise as one,
Under the watchful gaze of the sun.

In prayerful whispers, we connect,
Within our hearts, divine reflect.
From dusk to dawn, we journey wide,
The heart's horizon, our sacred guide.

Graceful Rebirth

From ancient dust, a rise anew,
Emerging light, a vibrant view.
In every ending, seeds are sown,
A graceful rebirth, life has shown.

Through trials faced, the spirit blooms,
In shadows cast, a light resumes.
In faith, we find our strength to grow,
Embracing change, the love we sow.

With every heartbeat, echoes sound,
In stillness, grace and peace abound.
Transformation's hand, so tender and dear,
Guides us onward, erasing fear.

The cycle turns, like seasons change,
From ashes rise, we rearrange.
In gratitude, we stand anew,
With open hearts, to life's great view.

For in the dance of life divine,
Each step we take, a sacred sign.
Renewed in spirit, whole and free,
We welcome forth our destiny.

The Song of Morning

Awake, O world, with joyful tune,
The morning sings of life's new bloom.
With every ray, hope's promise beams,
In the golden light, we weave our dreams.

The birds take flight on wings of grace,
In nature's choir, we find our place.
Each note a prayer, each sound a plea,
Together in sacred harmony.

As dew-kissed petals greet the sun,
A symphony from all has begun.
With open hearts and hands outstretched,
Embracing love, our lives are etched.

In stillness found, the spirit knows,
The beauty in each moment grows.
A canvas bright, painted with light,
In the song of morning, hearts take flight.

So rise, dear soul, and sing along,
In every breath, we share this song.
The morning dawns, a gift so rare,
In every heartbeat, love and care.

Embraced by the Whispering Winds

In the hush of dawn, a whisper sings,
The gentle breeze, on sacred wings.
It carries prayers to skies so wide,
Embraced by the winds, the soul's sweet guide.

Each rustling leaf, a voice divine,
In nature's choir, our hearts entwine.
God's wisdom flows, a soft caress,
In the whispering winds, we find our rest.

Through valleys deep, we hear the call,
In trials faced, we shall not fall.
With every breath, we breathe in grace,
Embraced by the winds, we find our place.

From mountain peaks to oceans vast,
In sacred moments, shadows cast.
The winds remind us, we are seen,
In every gust, His love we glean.

So let us dance upon this earth,
In harmony, we find our worth.
With every whisper, let us rise,
Embraced by the winds, we touch the skies.

Streams of Hope Flowing Upward

In fields where sorrows gently lie,
The streams of hope begin to sigh.
They rise like visions, pure and clear,
Flowing upward, drawing near.

Each droplet glimmers in the light,
A promise made, a beacon bright.
Through trials faced, we find our peace,
Streams of hope that never cease.

As rivers carve their path so bold,
Our spirits soar, our hearts unfold.
With faith as strong as ancient trees,
In streams of hope, our souls find ease.

Let not the shadows steal your gaze,
For in His hands, our hopes we'll raise.
Through every storm, each doubt and fear,
Streams of hope flow ever near.

So drink from wells of love divine,
Through streams of hope, our hearts align.
Together we rise, forever free,
Flowing upward, eternally.

Unfolding Wings of Faith

Beneath the stars, our spirits soar,
With every breath, we seek for more.
Unfolding wings, we rise above,
In trails of light, we find His love.

The sky, a canvas, bright and wide,
With whispered dreams, we cannot hide.
In every trial, we learn to trust,
Unfolding wings, in faith we must.

Eagles flying through tempest wild,
In faith's embrace, we are His child.
Through storms of life, we lift our eyes,
Unfolding wings, we learn to rise.

With hearts aflame, our spirits yearn,
To grasp the fire, for which we burn.
In unity, our voices sing,
Unfolding wings, to Him we cling.

So let us soar, both high and free,
In faith's embrace, we'll always be.
Through every journey, guide our way,
Unfolding wings, come what may.

The Eternal Bloom of the Heart

In gardens vast, where love is sown,
The eternal bloom, a grace we've known.
From soil rich to skies of blue,
The heart's flower, forever true.

With petals soft, and fragrance sweet,
Each blossom waits where faith and hope meet.
In every storm, it stands so tall,
The eternal bloom, it shall not fall.

Through seasons change, it learns to grow,
In light and shadow, love's warm glow.
With every sunset, the colors blend,
The eternal bloom, our truest friend.

So let us cherish what blooms inside,
With faith as roots, love as our guide.
In every heart, this truth we find,
The eternal bloom of the heart, divine.

Together we rise, hand in hand,
With love as threads in a sacred strand.
In the garden of grace, we joyfully start,
The eternal bloom of the heart.

Silent Hymns of Hope

In the quiet dawn, we rise,
Voices meld in softest prayer,
Hearts entwined with faith's embrace,
Guided by the light we share.

Whispers of love, gently flow,
Through valleys deep, o'er mountains high,
Every tear and every sigh,
Transforming pain to sacred glow.

Stars above in velvet night,
Twinkling with a promise near,
In the stillness, find our strength,
For in our faith, we persevere.

Hands uplifted, eyes aglow,
Together, we will stand as one,
In each moment, grace will bloom,
A testament of what's to come.

For in the silence, hope resounds,
With every heartbeat, truth is found,
In the quiet, peace awake,
Silent hymns for love's sweet sake.

The Embrace of Eternity

In the stillness of the night,
We find solace in the stars,
Every heartbeat, every breath,
A whisper of life's gentle scars.

Time flows like a river wide,
Each moment wrapped in sacred grace,
In the embrace of eternity,
We gather strength in love's embrace.

Golden dawn brings warmth anew,
Casting shadows on our fears,
In the light, we find our path,
Through laughter, joy, and solemn tears.

Faith, a beacon shining bright,
Guiding souls through darkest days,
In the love that knows no end,
We journey forth in holy ways.

In the circle of this life,
Every soul a shining part,
Together, we shall weave the thread,
Of love eternal in each heart.

Journeying Toward the Infinite

Upon the road where shadows play,
With every step, we seek the light,
Hearts aligned with purpose bold,
Journeying onward, day and night.

Mountains high and valleys low,
We tread the paths our souls have made,
In every challenge we will grow,
Strengthened by the love displayed.

Through stormy skies and gentle breeze,
Every trial, a lesson learned,
The fire within that never fades,
Ignites the passion, fervor turned.

In the silence, wisdom speaks,
Offering grace with every breath,
Together, we will carry on,
Embracing life, defying death.

As stars align on destiny's path,
We trust in what the heart can see,
For every journey brings us home,
Toward the infinite, we are free.

The Glory of the Morning

In the morning's tender glow,
Daybreak whispers, hope revived,
With every sunbeam's golden touch,
New beginnings come alive.

Birds take flight in azure skies,
Their songs a sweet, melodious hymn,
With nature's chorus, we unite,
In praise of life, our spirits brim.

Through fields of grace, we wander wide,
Finding joy in every stride,
In the glory of creation's hand,
A sacred truth we cannot hide.

As light cascades on every bloom,
Each petal holds a prayer of peace,
In the warmth of love's embrace,
All burdens lift, and sorrows cease.

Let every morning be our guide,
To seek the miracle of here,
For in the glory of each day,
Hope is born, and love draws near.

The Light of Mercy

In shadows deep, Thy mercy glows,
A gentle light where love bestows.
Through trials faced, we seek Thy grace,
In every heart, a holy space.

With open arms, we turn to Thee,
In moments lost, You set us free.
Forgiveness shines, a radiant beam,
Awakening faith, igniting the dream.

O gracious Lord, our refuge pure,
In every storm, Thy peace, we cure.
With prayers uplifted, we humbly call,
For in Thy mercy, we rise and fall.

Let love abound, let hope arise,
In hearts transformed, the spirit flies.
A sacred path, abundant life,
In the light of mercy, banish strife.

Eternal light that guides our way,
Within Your arms, we wish to stay.
Forever bound in love's embrace,
O Lord of mercy, our saving grace.

Sacred Ascent

To heights unknown, we seek to climb,
In faith's embrace, we leave all time.
With every step, a hymn we raise,
In sacred light, we seek to blaze.

The mountain calls, so steep and grand,
A journey led by Your strong hand.
Through valleys low, our spirits soar,
In trials faced, we find the door.

O gentle Guide, through fire and rain,
You lift us up, erase the pain.
With love as fuel, we strive to rise,
We touch the heavens, paint the skies.

In unity, our hearts are bound,
Each whispered prayer, a sacred sound.
Together we ascend the throne,
In the arms of grace, we find our home.

At every peak, Your glory shines,
In quietude, our soul's aligns.
With courage bright, through storms we tread,
On sacred ascent, by faith we're led.

In the Garden of the Divine

In the garden where beauty blooms,
With fragrant hope, our spirit resumes.
Each petal bright, a prayer sincere,
In the divine embrace, we draw near.

The gentle breeze, Your whisper sweet,
In Your presence, our hearts repeat.
O tranquil shade, where peace is found,
In sacred silence, love abounds.

With hands uplifted, we sow the seeds,
In faith's rich soil, our longing leads.
Together we nurture, love will grow,
In the garden's heart, Your glory we know.

Each season turns, with grace we thrive,
In every trial, we feel alive.
The fruits of spirit, ripe and true,
In the garden of the divine, renew.

Through winding paths, we journey forth,
In every dawn, we find our worth.
With joy and sorrow, both entwined,
In the garden's light, our souls aligned.

Threads of Hope

In woven dreams, the fabric holds,
A tapestry of stories told.
Each thread a prayer, a whispered sigh,
In hope we trust, we reach for the sky.

With every struggle, threads entwine,
Through darkness faced, Your light we find.
In unity, our hearts are sewn,
With courage bright, we stand as one.

O faithful Weaver, guide our way,
Through trials faced, we brightly stay.
In love's embrace, our spirits mend,
With threads of hope, we will not bend.

As colors blend, we rise anew,
In grace renewed, our faith shines true.
With every heartbeat, every breath,
We weave a story that conquers death.

In life's great loom, with hands outspread,
In every moment, hope is fed.
A masterpiece, our lives compose,
In threads of hope, our spirit grows.

The Radiance of Hope

In shadows cast by doubt and fear,
A light emerges, shining clear.
With whispered grace, it calls us near,
Embrace the warmth, let love endear.

Through trials faced and burdens borne,
Each heart restored, new life is worn.
The path of faith, though sometimes worn,
Leads forth to dawn, a day reborn.

With every tear, a lesson found,
In darkened moments, hope's profound.
A guiding star, forever sound,
In sacred trust, our spirits bound.

So lift your gaze, let worries cease,
In every struggle, find your peace.
With open arms, let prayers release,
The radiance of hope, sweet solace, cease.

Waters of Renewal

In quiet streams, the blessings flow,
With gentle hands, our spirits grow.
Each drop a gift, a vibrant glow,
Cleansed by the waters, love we sow.

Beneath the sky, the heavens weep,
Their tears transform, the soul's deep keep.
In every current, promises sweep,
A sacred dance, where dreams do leap.

The river's song, a balm for woes,
In every wave, the spirit knows.
As nature's voice in silence grows,
Rebirth awaits, where faith bestows.

So drink the waters, pure and bright,
Let currents guide you towards the light.
In every moment, hold on tight,
For in renewal, hearts take flight.

Climbing Sacred Peaks

Behold the heights where mountain crowns,
With every step, shake off the frowns.
Through trials faced, no soul abounds,
In faith we rise, where grace surrounds.

The air is thin, the path is steep,
Yet onward we tread, our promise keep.
In silence deep, our spirits leap,
From every summit, blessings seep.

The sun will rise, the dawn will break,
Each victory claimed, no heart will quake.
In unity, the bonds we make,
To climb these peaks, for love's own sake.

So lift your eyes to skies above,
For in each challenge grows our love.
With every heart, let courage shove,
We climb the sacred peaks thereof.

In the Embrace of the Divine

In quiet moments, breathe Him in,
The softest whisper, where love begins.
With open hearts, let healing spin,
In the embrace, we lose our sin.

A sacred bond, a tender touch,
In every prayer, we feel so much.
With every soul, the heavens clutch,
In every trial, His love is such.

The nightingale sings, in sweet refrain,
A melody to lift the pain.
In joy or sorrow, our hearts remain,
In the embrace, we break the chain.

So cherish moments, grace divine,
In every heartbeat, love does shine.
With every prayer, our lives entwine,
In the embrace of the Divine.

The Dance of the Divine

In the silence of the night,
Stars awaken with gentle light.
Angels whisper, soft as air,
Heaven's music, beyond compare.

In rhythm with the sacred throng,
Hearts unite in blessed song.
Steps of joy, a holy trance,
Round we go in love's great dance.

The Creator's touch, divine and clear,
Guiding souls who gather near.
In the presence, feel the glow,
In every heartbeat, love will flow.

With every twirl, our spirits rise,
Lifted up to meet the skies.
In this dance, we find our place,
Lost in the warmth of boundless grace.

Together in this sacred space,
We celebrate the human race.
Hand in hand, we share the light,
Forever blessed, our souls take flight.

Embers of Grace

In the ashes of the night,
Faintly glimmer, embers bright.
From the struggles, hope will rise,
Grace emerges to fill the skies.

Fires of love, igniting peace,
Through the trials, hearts find ease.
In the darkness, truth will shine,
Embers glow, a sign divine.

Each moment, a chance to grow,
In the warmth, our spirits flow.
With trust in all that we can't see,
Embers guide us, setting free.

Gather close, let warmth embrace,
In the quiet, feel His grace.
Through the storm, we'll find our way,
Embers of grace, here to stay.

As the night fades into dawn,
Hope ignites, the fear is gone.
With every ember, faith will blend,
In grace's light, our hearts ascend.

Garlands of Trust

On the path where shadows lie,
Garlands woven, hearts held high.
With each step, we learn and grow,
Trust in love, the way to go.

Binding souls with threads of light,
In the day and in the night.
Faithful hearts, together strong,
In this journey, we belong.

Through the trials, we find grace,
Trusting in the sacred space.
Every challenge, a chance to rise,
Garlands forming as we prize.

In each moment, knowledge blooms,
Dispelling fears, erasing glooms.
With open hearts, let love abound,
Garlands of trust can always be found.

Together on this sacred path,
In love's embrace, we feel the wrath.
Yet through each storm, we see the light,
Garlands of trust will win the fight.

The Fruit of Faith

In the orchard, ripe and true,
Faith of old brings blessings new.
Each blossom whispers of the grace,
In every heart, a sacred place.

With open hands, we gather round,
The fruit of faith, in joy, is found.
In the garden, growth will show,
Seeds of love begin to sow.

Through the seasons, trials met,
Harvests come, no need for fret.
Each sacrifice bears sweet reward,
The fruit of faith, our true accord.

In each bite, a story told,
Of faith and love, so brave and bold.
With grateful hearts, we lift our praise,
For every fruit, our soul's embrace.

In the twilight, shadows grow,
Yet in the dark, our faith will glow.
Together, we rejoice and sing,
The fruit of faith, our offering.

In the Shadow of Sacred Peaks

In the stillness of dawn's light,
Whispers of faith take flight.
Mountains rise, steadfast and grand,
Guiding souls with a gentle hand.

Under the vast, empyrean dome,
Hearts find solace, a sacred home.
Prayerful breaths fill the air,
In the shadow, we "cast away care."

Every stone holds a story untold,
Of seekers brave, courageous and bold.
In reverence, their knees shall bend,
As nature and spirit beautifully blend.

Streams of grace through valleys flow,
Kindling hope for those below.
In unity we stand, strong and free,
In the light of His majesty.

Together in harmony, hearts entwined,
We rise in faith, our souls aligned.
In mountain shadows, whispers pray,
Guided by love, we find our way.

Blossoming in Prayerful Heights

In gardens where the angels dwell,
Each petal tells a tale to tell.
With every prayer, a seed is sown,
In prayerful heights, His love is known.

Branches stretch toward the heavenly sky,
Where praise and worship never die.
Colors burst, ablaze with grace,
In this sacred, holy space.

Birds sing hymns of joy and peace,
In nature's choir, our hearts release.
Each note a prayer, unique and bright,
Illuminating the dark with light.

With each dawn, new blessings flow,
In radiant blooms, the spirit grows.
In every fragrance, a promise clear,
God's embrace, forever near.

In silence, we hear the soft refrain,
A melody sung through joy and pain.
Blossoming hearts in sacred flight,
In prayerful heights, we feel His light.

The Sacred Symphony of Ascent

In echoes loud, the heavens sing,
A symphony that souls bring.
Each note a prayer rising high,
Reaching out to the endless sky.

With every heartbeat, a sacred call,
In unity, we rise, we fall.
Collective voices traverse the way,
Finding strength in night and day.

Mountains resonate with sacred sound,
In the stillness, hope is found.
Harmony birthed from every heart,
In life's journey, we play our part.

Every tear, a note in the song,
Together in faith, we all belong.
In the symphony of light and shade,
Our spirits dance as prayers cascade.

Ascending higher with each refrain,
In sacred spaces, we are not in vain.
United in love, we climb the steep,
In the symphony, our souls shall leap.

Elysian Echoes of the Heart

In the gentle hush of twilight's grace,
Elysian echoes in every place.
Songs of the heart rise like the stars,
Uniting the lost with the ones afar.

In the warmth of love's embrace,
Faith surrounds us, a sacred space.
With open arms, we seek the divine,
In every heartbeat, love shall shine.

Soft whispers guide the weary soul,
In grace, we find ourselves made whole.
The tapestry of fate intertwines,
Crafted through joys and struggles that bind.

Beauty lies in the journey we tread,
With hope in our hearts and light overhead.
In brokenness, we mend and grow,
Elysian echoes forever flow.

As night gives way to the dawn's soft glow,
We rise together, with love to bestow.
In echoes of faith, we play our part,
In the sacred rhythm of the heart.

Radiance of the Spirit's Ascent

In quietude, the soul will rise,
A whisper carried through the skies.
Each breath a prayer, a gentle sigh,
In love's embrace, we learn to fly.

The light within, a sacred flame,
Guiding hearts, calling each name.
With faith as wings, we reach the stars,
Together woven, despite our scars.

In stillness, find the strength anew,
The path ahead, so bright, so true.
With every step, the shadows flee,
In the spirit's glow, we are set free.

Through trials faced, through joy and pain,
The spirit climbs, the heart's refrain.
In unity, we journey forth,
The radiance of our sacred worth.

Let laughter echo, let love take flight,
In every day, there shines a light.
The spirit soars, a quest divine,
In grace and peace, our hearts entwine.

In the Embrace of Morning's Glow

Awake, O heart, to dawn's soft light,
In morning's glow, all feels so right.
The world renewed, each leaf and flower,
In nature's arms, we find power.

The birds sing hymns of joy, so free,
A gentle whisper calls to me.
In every hue, a promise lies,
As truth unfolds beneath the skies.

The quiet grace of dawn's first breath,
A moment rife with life and depth.
In stillness, find the sacred thread,
The path of love, where hearts are led.

In prayerful silence, souls unite,
In morning's glow, we seek the light.
With gratitude, we rise again,
In every heartbeat, love's refrain.

Let each new dawn our spirits lift,
As blessings come, our greatest gift.
In the embrace of hope's warm ray,
We walk together, come what may.

A Pilgrim's Graceful Voyage

Upon the road, a pilgrim's quest,
With every step, the soul finds rest.
Through valleys deep and mountains high,
In faith, our spirits learn to fly.

The path is long, but endless grace,
In every trial, a holy place.
As footprints mark the sacred ground,
In unity, our hearts are found.

With guiding stars that shine above,
The journey leads to wisdom's love.
In silence speaks the truth so clear,
As we embrace what we hold dear.

Through storms that come and shadows cast,
The pilgrim's heart beats strong and fast.
In gentle whispers, hope ignites,
A beacon shining through the nights.

So onward we tread, hand in hand,
In fellowship, we understand.
A pilgrimage of grace and light,
Together, we ascend to heights.

Finding Solace in Heavenly Heights

In silent prayer, we seek the skies,
Where peace and love forever lies.
The mountains echo, the valleys sing,
In harmony, our spirits cling.

With every breath, a sacred chance,
In nature's arms, our hearts will dance.
The clouds embrace, the heavens glow,
In stillness, we let our worries go.

Ascend with faith, our burdens shed,
In trust we rise, by grace we're led.
Through trials faced, our spirits soar,
In heavenly heights, we seek for more.

Let every moment be a prayer,
As love surrounds, we find we care.
In gentle light, we find our way,
With open hearts, come what may.

So here we stand, both strong and meek,
In unity, the truth we seek.
Finding solace, hearts entwined,
In heavenly heights, our souls aligned.

When the Heart Takes Flight

In whispers soft, the spirit calls,
Where shadows fade, and light enthralls.
The fervent wish, a sacred prayer,
To rise above, with love laid bare.

On wings of faith, we lift our gaze,
Through trials deep, we find our ways.
In every beat, a promise new,
The heart's embrace, our souls pursue.

When burdens heavy weigh us down,
In trust we find our sacred crown.
A journey paved with kindness bright,
In silence found, the heart takes flight.

Through storms that roar and skies that weep,
In God's embrace, our spirits leap.
Transcending all that doubt may bring,
A melody, the angels sing.

The stars align, a guiding light,
In darkest hours, we seek the right.
With every tear, a joy ignites,
In unity, our hearts unite.

The Horizon of Spiritual Renewal

Upon the dawn, where shadows blend,
A promise blooms, the soul will mend.
With open hearts, we greet the day,
In gratitude, we find our way.

The clouds disperse, a vision clear,
In stillness lies what we hold dear.
A sacred bond, a light revealed,
Through faith's embrace, our wounds are healed.

The horizon calls with colors bright,
In every hue, the love ignites.
As whispers rise on gentle breeze,
We find our rest, our hearts at ease.

In sacred circles, peace unfolds,
A tapestry of stories told.
With hands outstretched, we share divine,
In every soul, a spark will shine.

With every step, a chance to grow,
Through trials faced, our spirits sow.
In sacred trust, we journey far,
Our lights combined, the guiding star.

Ascending Through the Veils of Grace

In whispers low, the angels sing,
Of grace that comes through everything.
Enfolded in compassion's cloak,
A gentle push, the heart awoke.

Through every veil, a deepened breath,
We rise above the fear of death.
With hope as guide, we climb the heights,
In love's embrace, the soul ignites.

In every trial, a lesson found,
In stillness deep, our peace is crowned.
A sacred path of trust we trace,
With every step, we find our place.

The veils of doubt begin to part,
In faith's embrace, we feel the start.
A journey vast, a quest for light,
Ascending high, our spirits bright.

In every moment, grace bestowed,
Through faith and love, our hearts are flowed.
A melody of truths set free,
In unity, we're meant to be.

Ethereal Pathways of the Heart

In sacred silence, whispers known,
Ethereal pathways softly grown.
Each step we take, a dance with grace,
In love's embrace, we find our space.

With every heartbeat, truth unfolds,
A tapestry of stories told.
In fragile moments, strength we claim,
United souls, we fan the flame.

The light within begins to shine,
A sacred bond, forever mine.
Through valleys deep and mountains high,
Together, we will touch the sky.

In every soul, a light divine,
An echo of the love we find.
With open hands, we share our part,
In ethereal pathways of the heart.

As dawn breaks through with colors bright,
In unity, we seek the light.
With faith in heart, we move as one,
In love's embrace, our journey's begun.

Between Heaven and Earth

In twilight's grace, souls entwine,
Bound by love, both yours and mine.
Angels sing from above so clear,
Guiding hearts, dispelling fear.

With each breath, we rise and soar,
Seeking peace forevermore.
Hands uplifted, we lift prayer,
With faith unwavering, we share.

The stars align, a sacred dance,
In harmony, we find our chance.
Beneath the moon's soft, silver hue,
God whispers softly, "I am you."

Nature's hymn, a holy song,
In every moment, we belong.
Together still, our spirits roam,
In between, we find our home.

Each dawn presents a brand new way,
To witness grace in light of day.
With every sunset, hope is born,
In the twilight, souls are worn.

Communion with the Light

In stillness found, the spirit calls,
Echoes of love in sacred halls.
Hearts united, we stand in grace,
Together seeking a holy place.

With eyes closed tight, we feel the night,
The warmth of peace, a guiding light.
In quiet moments, whispers flow,
And in the dark, faith starts to grow.

Lifting praises, our voices blend,
A symphony that will not end.
In every heartbeat, prayers arise,
To touch the heavens, to reach the skies.

The light within, forever shines,
Connecting souls through sacred lines.
With open hearts, we come to see,
In union's bond, we're truly free.

With every dawn, a gift so bright,
A dance of shadows, a dance of light.
In communion, souls find delight,
Eternal beauty in endless flight.

Hearts ablaze with holy fire,
We seek the truth, our one desire.
In endless love, we are reborn,
Finding strength in every morn.

Lifting Hearts in Harmony

In the stillness, love prevails,
A soft whisper as faith sails.
Together now, our spirits rise,
In sacred union, we touch the skies.

With voices lifted, we share the song,
In every note, we all belong.
The melody of life feels clear,
In harmony, we cast out fear.

Through trials faced, we stand as one,
In every challenge, love's never done.
With open arms, the world we greet,
In every heartbeat, love's retreat.

Within the silence, truth reveals,
The heart of faith, the soul it heals.
In every moment, hope resides,
As we uplift, our spirit guides.

Beneath the stars, we find our way,
In every dawn, a brand new day.
Together still, we forge our path,
In love's embrace, we find the math.

With joy as pure as morning dew,
We dance in light, forever true.
In every breath, a sacred vow,
Lifting hearts, we sing our how.

Whispers of the Eternal

In the silence, a secret breathes,
Telling tales of ancient leaves.
The winds carry what time forgot,
In every whisper, truth is sought.

As dawn unfolds its golden wings,
Nature sings of sacred things.
Every creature plays its part,
Reminding us of the Creator's heart.

Through valleys deep and mountains high,
We hear a voice that will not die.
It calls us forth, ignites the flame,
In every soul, it speaks our name.

In every sunset, is a kiss,
A gentle touch, a moment's bliss.
With every star that lights the sky,
A promise whispered, "Do not cry."

Through trials faced, and storms endured,
The heart finds strength that is assured.
In whispers soft, we feel the near,
The eternal love that draws us here.

With each heartbeat, a prayer unfolds,
Stories of faith that time upholds.
In the depths of night, in light of morn,
We find the path in which we're born.

The Call of Ascendance

In the quiet of the morning light,
The spirit stirs, a sacred flight.
Whispers of hope dance in the air,
Calling the hearts that seek and care.

With every step upon this path,
We shed our doubts, embraced by wrath.
Lifted by angels, guided by grace,
We rise above, in this holy space.

Ascend, oh souls, to heights divine,
Through trials faced, we intertwine.
Faith as our banner, love as our shield,
In this promise, our hearts are healed.

Through shadows deep, we find the way,
In each quiet prayer, in each soul's sway.
Embracing the light, we trust the call,
Together we rise, together we fall.

At the dawn of a brand new day,
We find our purpose, come what may.
In unity strong, we write our song,
The call of ascendance, forever long.

Patrons of the Sky

Beneath the vast and endless blue,
We gather our hearts, pure and true.
Patrons above, we seek your light,
Guide our spirits, through the night.

The stars are sentinels, shining bright,
Bearing witness to our flight.
In each twinkle, a whisper shows,
The love of the heavens in soft repose.

We lift our prayers like incense high,
As angels hover, wings in the sky.
Through the storms, we find our way,
Patrons of the sky, hear what we say.

In moments of doubt, when spirits wane,
We turn to you to ease our pain.
The grace of the heavens fills our souls,
As we journey forth, seeking our goals.

With eyes uplifted, we stand as one,
Trusting the guidance of the sun.
In sacred circles, our dreams ignite,
Patrons of the sky, forever in sight.

Unfolding Wings of Faith

In the depths of our quiet hearts,
Faith emerges, a work of art.
Unfolding wings, we dare to soar,
Embracing love, forevermore.

Through trials faced and burdens borne,
In every tear, a new hope is sworn.
Lifted and carried on winds so pure,
Unfolding wings, we shall endure.

The journey is long, yet still we rise,
Guided by love, beneath vast skies.
Each moment a treasure, each breath a grace,
In the arms of faith, we find our place.

With courage ignited, in hearts ablaze,
We walk the path, through life's maze.
Unfolding wings, no fear can bind,
In the light of truth, our souls aligned.

As we take flight, a vision clear,
Faith as our anchor, love our spear.
Together we soar, unshackled and free,
Unfolding wings of faith, eternity.

Blossom Amidst the Storm

When tempests rage and skies turn gray,
We find our strength in words we say.
Blossom amidst the storms we face,
With roots of hope, in sacred grace.

The rain may fall, but we stand tall,
With petals soft, we answer the call.
In the fury, we learn to thrive,
Through every challenge, we come alive.

The thorns remind us of love's sweet cost,
Yet through the struggle, we are not lost.
Embracing the chaos, we bloom anew,
In the heart of the storm, we find our view.

Each gust a lesson, each drop a song,
In unity strong, we will belong.
Blossom amidst the shadows cast,
For even in darkness, the light holds fast.

When the sun breaks through, and warm winds call,
We gather our petals, we stand tall.
In the garden of life where blessings wait,
Blossom amidst the storm, we celebrate.

The Chosen Path

In silent prayer, we tread the way,
Guided by light, unseen each day.
Choices laid bare, like stones in stream,
We walk in faith, embracing the dream.

With every step, our spirits rise,
Trusting the path, beneath vast skies.
Through trials faced, we learn to see,
The grace bestowed, forever free.

Hearts entwined in sacred trust,
A journey adorned with hope and dust.
In shadows deep, we find our song,
For on this path, we all belong.

The whispers call, from ancient wood,
Reminding us of all that's good.
With every turn, we seek the truth,
In wisdom gained, we find our youth.

So onward bound, let courage steer,
With love as guide, we banish fear.
For on this trail, in every breath,
We walk in light, defying death.

The Unfurling Blossom

In gentle grace, a flower wakes,
Petals embrace the sun that breaks.
Each drop of dew, like tears of joy,
A silent hymn, no heart can coy.

Roots buried deep in sacred ground,
From darkness sprout, new life is found.
The world holds breath, as colors bloom,
In harmony, dispelling gloom.

With every dawn, new hope ignites,
A dance of life on starry nights.
Unfolding dreams, we learn to trust,
In faith we rise, from earthly dust.

Nature's art speaks volumes true,
In every shade, a lively hue.
As seasons change, our spirits flow,
In love's embrace, we learn to grow.

So let us stand, in beauty's grace,
To find our light, our rightful place.
For in each blossom's tender grace,
Lies the reflection of divine space.

Lessons from the Sun

Awake each morn, the golden gleam,
A canvas bright, a radiant dream.
With open eyes, we greet the light,
Lessons learned in day and night.

The sun bestows its warming ray,
Dispelling doubts that cloud our way.
In shadows cast, we learn to see,
The power held in love's decree.

Each dawn a chance, a fresh new start,
To share the warmth, to mend the heart.
In fleeting time, we grasp the call,
To rise again, lest we should fall.

In twilight's glow, reflections shared,
For every burden, love has cared.
As sunsets paint the evening sky,
We find the strength to live, not die.

So cherish light, let it bestow,
The peace within, the seeds to grow.
In every beam, a message spun,
The greatest lessons come from sun.

The Altars of Our Souls

In quiet spaces, hearts laid bare,
We build our altars, deepened prayer.
With whispered hopes, we seek the grace,
In every soul, a sacred place.

With open hands, we lift our voice,
In unity, we make the choice.
For every tear that stains the ground,
Is love's embrace, forever found.

The flame of faith burns ever bright,
Illuminating darkest night.
In moments shared, we find our song,
Together strong, we right the wrong.

From ashes rise, with purpose true,
In every heart, a bond anew.
The altars stand, where spirits soar,
In love's embrace, forever more.

So let us nurture what we find,
In every heart, a truth aligned.
For on these altars, souls will meet,
In love's sweet dance, our lives complete.

Interwoven with the Divine

In the stillness, whispers dwell,
The sacred breath, we all can tell.
Threads of faith, interlace the night,
Heaven's tapestry, woven in light.

With every heartbeat, a prayer grows,
In gratitude, our spirit flows.
United souls, in a sacred dance,
The touch of grace, a sweet romance.

Mountains bow to the softest sighs,
In the heart's depths, love never lies.
Through trials faced, miracles thrive,
In the Divine's arms, we are alive.

The stars whisper secrets aglow,
Guiding the seeker through ebb and flow.
In silence, we hear the sacred call,
Interwoven with the Divine, we are all.

Together we rise, in heavenly grace,
Creating pathways to a sacred space.
With every step, we honor the way,
Interwoven with the Divine, night and day.

Transcendence in the Morning Light

As dawn breaks softly, shadows flee,
The whispers of hope, a sweet decree.
In golden hues, our spirits soar,
Transcendence beckons, forevermore.

With every ray, warmth does ignite,
Awakening souls to the Purest Light.
In the quiet, wisdom flows,
In morning's grace, the heart knows.

In gratitude, we rise anew,
With every breath, a sacred view.
The canvas of life, brushed with care,
Transcendence blooms in the peaceful air.

With open hearts, we seek the path,
In every moment, love's aftermath.
Transcending shadows, we'll surely find,
The morning's light embraced in kind.

Together we walk, through time so bright,
Transcendence whispers, day into night.
In every heartbeat, a love divine,
In the morning light, our souls align.

Wrapped in Celestial Embrace

Beneath the starlit, endless skies,
In quiet corners, our spirit flies.
Wrapped in love, the cosmos we trace,
Finding unity in a celestial embrace.

The moonlight dances on waters deep,
Cradling secrets that stars must keep.
In every touch, the universe sings,
Wrapped in celestial arms, love springs.

Through the ages, our stories weave,
In sacred trust, we ever believe.
Guided by light, where shadows cease,
In cosmic arms, we find our peace.

Together we journey, hand in hand,
On paths of light, our hearts expand.
In every echo, a gentle hue,
Wrapped in celestial love, we renew.

So let us wander through time and space,
With open hearts in this divine race.
Wrapped in celestial warmth and glow,
In love's embrace, together we grow.

Awe at the Summit of Being

Atop the heights, where silence reigns,
In the breath of mountains, nothing remains.
Awe swells in the heart, pure and bright,
At the summit of being, bathed in light.

The valleys below, like dreams unspun,
In the stillness, the journey begun.
With every step, divinity's beam,
Guiding our souls to the sacred dream.

In moments fleeting, eternity breathes,
The sacred whispers, the heart believes.
In the quiet, truth becomes known,
At the summit of being, love has grown.

Together we gather, spirits aligned,
In harmony, our souls intertwined.
A tapestry woven by hands unseen,
In awe at the summit, we are redeemed.

Let this journey lead to the heights above,
Where echoes of wisdom speak only of love.
At the summit of being, forever free,
In the grace of the universe, we shall be.

Milton Keynes UK
Ingram Content Group UK Ltd.
UKHW031321271124
451618UK00007B/147